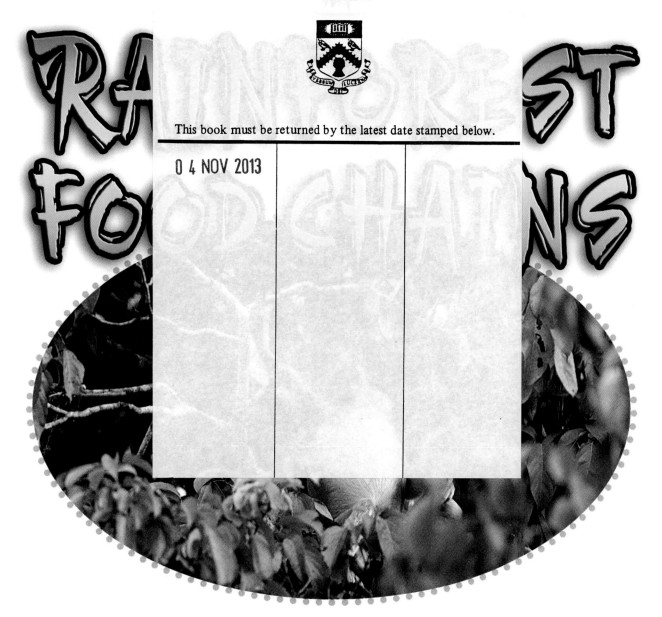

RAINFOREST FOOD CHAINS

Molly Aloian & Bobbie Kalman

🌴 Crabtree Publishing Company

www.crabtreebooks.com

Created by Bobbie Kalman

Dedicated by Crystal Sikkens
To my close friend, Alexis Vanderwier

Editor-in-Chief
Bobbie Kalman

Writing team
Molly Aloian
Bobbie Kalman

Substantive editor
Kathryn Smithyman

Editors
Michael Hodge
Robin Johnson
Kelley MacAulay
Rebecca Sjonger

Design
Katherine Berti
Margaret Amy Salter (cover)

Production coordinator
Heather Fitzpatrick

Photo research
Crystal Sikkens

Consultant
Patricia Loesche, Ph.D., Animal Behavior Program,
Department of Psychology, University of Washington

Illustrations
Barbara Bedell: pages 3 (leaves, lizard, and snake), 10 (top and middle), 11 (rhino,
    grasshopper, and leaves), 25 (ground and bacteria), 27 (frog, lizard, seeds, leaves,
    and grasshopper)
Katherine Berti: pages 3 (monkey, fruit on branch, and leopard), 10 (bottom),
    11 (leopard, monkey, tree, and fruit on branch), 12, 27 (leopard, monkey, and fruit)
Cori Marvin: page 3 (bat)
Bonna Rouse: pages 3 (flower-top, bird, beetle, and elephant), 9, 11 (bat), 27 (caterpillar)
Margaret Amy Salter: pages 3 (ant, butterfly, and flower on left), 6, 11 (flower),
    25 (magnifying glass and plant with roots)

Photographs
Bruce Coleman Inc.: Mark Taylor/Warren Photographic: page 7
iStockphoto.com: Mark Huntington: page 4
© Jurgen Freund/naturepl.com: page 16
Martin Harvey/NHPA: page 22
Photo Researchers, Inc.: Fletcher & Baylis: pages 14 (bottom), 15, 18; Jacques Jangoux: page 13
Visuals Unlimited: Tim Hauf: page 28; George Loun: pages 14 (top), 24; Inga Spence: page 29
Other images by Corel, Creatas, and Digital Vision

Library and Archives Canada Cataloguing in Publication

Aloian, Molly
    Rainforest food chains / Molly Aloian & Bobbie Kalman.

(Food chains)
Includes index.
ISBN-13: 978-0-7787-1951-9 (bound)
ISBN-13: 978-0-7787-1997-7 (pbk.)
ISBN-10: 0-7787-1951-0 (bound).--
ISBN-10: 0-7787-1997-9 (pbk.)
    1. Rain forest ecology--Juvenile literature. 2. Food chains
(Ecology)--Juvenile literature. 3. Rain forests--Juvenile literature.
I. Kalman, Bobbie, date. II. Title. III. Series: Food chains

QH541.5.R27A456 2006   j577.34'16   C2006-904918-1

Library of Congress Cataloging-in-Publication Data

Aloian, Molly.
    Rainforest food chains / Molly Aloian & Bobbie Kalman.
        p. cm. -- (Food chains)
    Includes index.
    ISBN-13: 978-0-7787-1951-9 (rlb)
    ISBN-10: 0-7787-1951-0 (rlb)
    ISBN-13: 978-0-7787-1997-7 (pb)
    ISBN-10: 0-7787-1997-9 (pb)
    1. Rain forest ecology--Juvenile literature. 2. Food chains (Ecology)--
Juvenile literature. 3. Rain forests--Juvenile literature.
I. Kalman, Bobbie. II. Title.
    QH541.5.R27A456 2007
    577.34'16--dc22
                                        2006020228

Crabtree Publishing Company

www.crabtreebooks.com   1-800-387-7650
Printed in the U.S.A./102012/CJ20120907

Published in Canada
Crabtree Publishing
616 Welland Ave.
St. Catharines, ON
L2M 5V6

Published in the United States
Crabtree Publishing
PMB 59051
350 Fifth Avenue, 59th Floor
New York, New York 10118

Published in the United Kingdom
Crabtree Publishing
Maritime House
Basin Road North, Hove
BN41 1WR

Published in Australia
Crabtree Publishing
3 Charles Street
Coburg North
VIC 3058

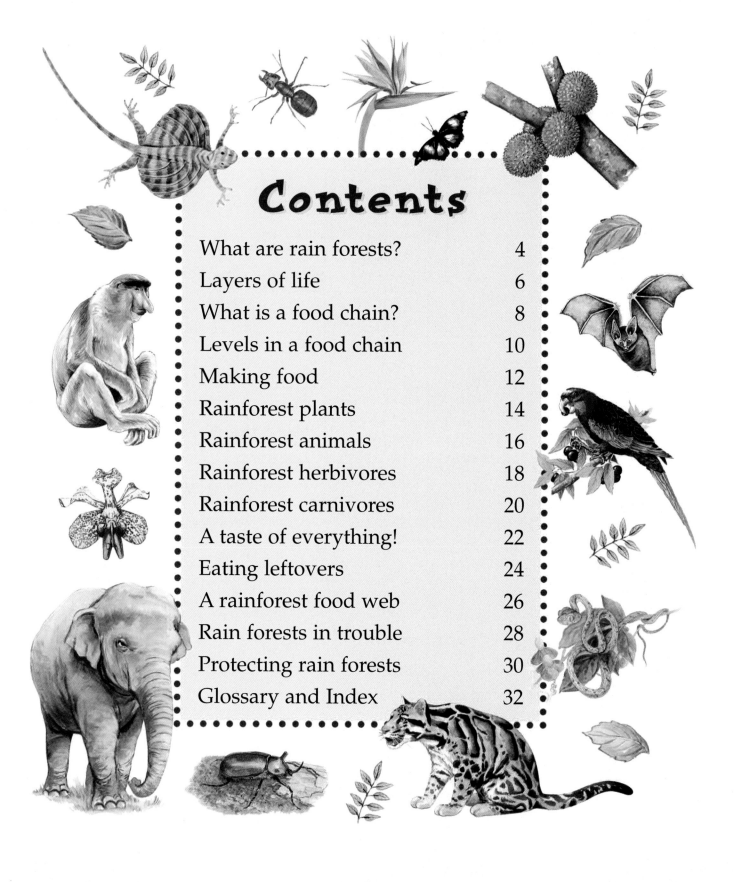

Contents

What are rain forests?	4
Layers of life	6
What is a food chain?	8
Levels in a food chain	10
Making food	12
Rainforest plants	14
Rainforest animals	16
Rainforest herbivores	18
Rainforest carnivores	20
A taste of everything!	22
Eating leftovers	24
A rainforest food web	26
Rain forests in trouble	28
Protecting rain forests	30
Glossary and Index	32

What are rain forests?

In tropical rain forests, it rains almost every day!

Rain forests are dense forests that contain many tall trees. Rain forests receive at least 100 inches (254 cm) of rain each year.

Two types

There are two main types of rain forests—**temperate rain forests** and **tropical rain forests**. Temperate rain forests are found in areas of the world that have hot summers and cold winters. Tropical rain forests are found near the **equator**, where the weather is warm year round. The equator is an imaginary line around the center of Earth.

Around the world

There are tropical rain forests in Central America, South America, Africa, Southeast Asia, and Australia. This book is about **food chains** in the tropical rain forests of Southeast Asia.

Plenty of life

Millions of **species**, or types, of plants and animals live in tropical rain forests. Plants and animals **thrive**, or grow well, in the hot, wet **climate**. Climate is the long-term weather conditions in an area. Climate includes temperature, rainfall, and wind. A lot of rain and sunshine cause many plants to grow. The plants provide food for many animals.

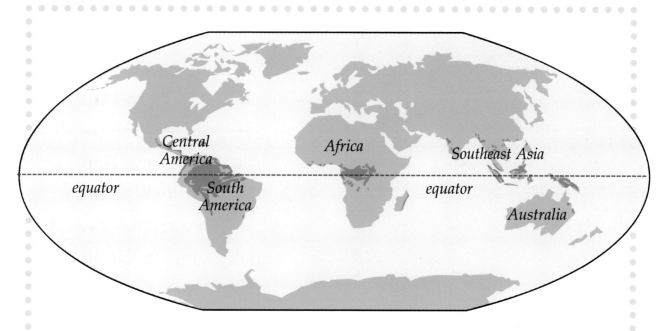

The dark green areas on this map show the locations of tropical rain forests on Earth. Tropical rain forests are near the equator. About one-quarter of the world's tropical rain forests are found in Southeast Asia. The temperatures in these rain forests are usually between 68° F and 95° F (20° C-35° C).

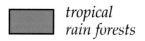
tropical rain forests

Layers of life

Like all forests, tropical rain forests are divided into four main layers. Different plants and animals live in each layer.

*The first layer of a rain forest is called the **emergent layer**. The emergent layer is made up of the tops of tall trees. Some trees are over 250 feet (76 m) tall, so they receive a lot of sunlight. Birds and bats live in this layer.*

emergent layer

canopy

understory

forest floor

*The second layer of a rain forest is called the **canopy**. The canopy is made up of the tops of shorter trees, most of which are between ten and 40 feet (3-12 m) tall. Many animals live in the canopy because there is plenty of food there. The trees in the canopy also receive a lot of sunlight.*

*The third layer is called the **understory**. This layer is made up of shorter trees, vines, and other plants. It is home to many animals. The emergent and canopy layers cover much of the understory, so this layer receives little sunlight.*

*The fourth layer is called the **forest floor**. This layer is at the bottom of a rain forest. It is always dark and shaded. Few plants grow on the forest floor, but many animals live there.*

Tree protection

The treetops in the canopy are thick and grow close together. They protect the understory and the forest floor from the hot sun. The shade from the canopy keeps the **soil**, or upper layer of earth, on the forest floor from becoming too dry. The canopy also shields the understory and forest floor from heavy rains and strong winds. These weather conditions can damage the plants that live in the lower layers.

Through gaps in the canopy, a little sunlight reaches the understory.

What is a food chain?

This orangutan needs water to stay alive.

This thorny phasmid is getting nutrients from the plant it is eating.

There are many living things in tropical rain forests. Plants and animals are living things. Plants and animals need food, water, air, and sunlight to stay alive.

Energy in food

Food contains **nutrients**. Plants and animals need nutrients to grow and to stay healthy. They get nutrients from food. Plants and animals also get **energy** from food. Plants need energy to grow. Animals need energy to breathe, to grow, to move from place to place, and to find food.

The sun's energy

Plants are the only living things that can make their own food! To make food, plants use energy from the sun.

Animals must eat

Animals cannot make food the way plants can. Animals must eat food to get nutrients and energy. Different animals eat different foods. Some animals eat plants. Others eat animals. Some animals eat both plants and animals. When animals eat other living things, food chains are formed. Look at the diagram on the right to see how a food chain works.

Using energy

Green plants trap the sun's energy and use it to make food. They use some of the energy as food and store the rest.

sun

plant

When an animal such as an insect eats a plant, it gets the energy that was stored in the plant. The insect does not get as much of the sun's energy as the plant received.

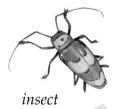

insect

When a frog eats an insect, energy is passed to the frog through the insect. The frog gets less of the sun's energy than the amount the insect received.

frog

Levels in a food chain

Every food chain has three levels. Plants make up the first level. Animals that eat plants make up the second level. Animals that eat other animals make up the third level.

Plants make food

Plants are **primary producers**. They are the **primary**, or first, living things in a food chain. They **produce**, or make, food for themselves. All plants store the food they do not use as energy.

Eating plants

The second level of a food chain is made up of **herbivores**. Herbivores are animals that eat plants. They are also called **primary consumers** because they are the first living things in a food chain to **consume**, or eat, food. When they eat plants, herbivores receive some of the energy stored in the plants.

Eating meat

The third level of a food chain is made up of **carnivores**, or animals that eat other animals. Carnivores are also called **secondary consumers**. They are the second group of living things in a food chain that eat food to get energy. Secondary consumers receive only small amounts of the sun's energy from their food.

The energy pyramid

The movement of energy through a food chain is shown in this **energy pyramid**. There are many plants at the first level of a food chain, so the first level of the energy pyramid is wide.

The second level is narrower than the first because there are fewer herbivores than there are plants. The top level of the pyramid is the narrowest because there are fewer carnivores than there are herbivores in a food chain.

Making food

Plants make food through a process called **photosynthesis**. Green plants contain a **pigment**, or color, called **chlorophyll**. Chlorophyll takes in energy from the sun and combines it with water, nutrients, and **carbon dioxide** to make food. Carbon dioxide is a gas in air.

Good glucose

The food plants make is a type of sugar called **glucose**. As plants make glucose, they release **oxygen**. Oxygen is another gas in air. Living things need oxygen to stay alive.

Tropical rain forests contain many green plants. As a result, rain forests release more oxygen during photosynthesis than do other types of forests.

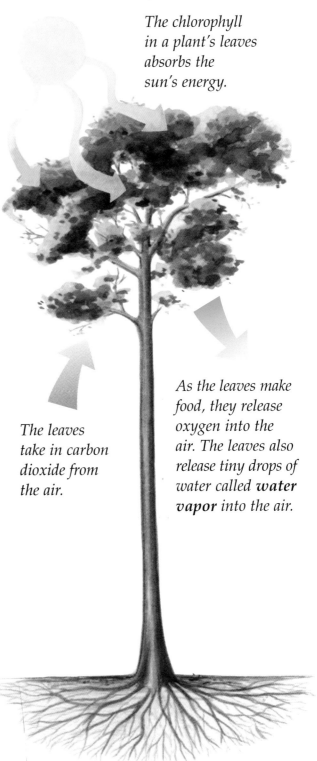

The chlorophyll in a plant's leaves absorbs the sun's energy.

*As the leaves make food, they release oxygen into the air. The leaves also release tiny drops of water called **water vapor** into the air.*

The leaves take in carbon dioxide from the air.

Maintaining moisture

During photosynthesis, rainforest trees and other plants absorb a lot of moisture through their roots. Rainforest plants also release moisture through their leaves during photosynthesis. By releasing moisture, the trees help maintain the wet conditions in tropical rain forests. The moisture helps more plants grow.

Removing and releasing

Large amounts of carbon dioxide are harmful to living things. During photosynthesis, rainforest plants remove carbon dioxide from the air. They store some carbon dioxide in their roots and stems and turn the rest into oxygen. Rain forests release huge amounts of oxygen into the air. Without rain forests, there would be too much carbon dioxide and not enough oxygen on Earth!

The large trees in this rain forest release moisture, which helps the smaller palm trees grow.

Rainforest plants

Many rainforest plants have **adapted**, or changed, in ways that help them survive in their **habitat**. These pages show some of the ways that rainforest plants have adapted.

*The leaves of many rainforest plants have long, narrow tips called **drip tips**. Drip tips allow water to trickle off the leaves. They protect the leaves from becoming damaged by too much water.*

Get into the groove

An **epiphyte**, shown right, is a plant that grows on another plant. In tropical rain forests, many epiphytes grow in the cracks or grooves on trees. There are often leaves and animal waste in these cracks, which provide the epiphytes with nutrients. The epiphytes need nutrients to grow. Epiphytes also absorb nutrients from the air and water. Many epiphytes grow on tall trees in order to reach sunlight in the canopy.

*The plants on which epiphytes grow are called **hosts**.*

Large and green

The treetops in the canopy block a lot of sunlight from reaching the understory and the forest floor. Many of the plants in the shaded, lower layers of the rain forest have adapted to survive with little light. The leaves on these plants are large and contain a lot of chlorophyll. The chlorophyll makes the leaves dark green. Large, dark-green leaves are better able to take in the little sunlight that is available.

The large leaves on the plants in the lower parts of rain forests are sometimes slanted or turned in ways that allow them to take in as much sunlight as possible.

Rainforest soil

There is not a lot of soil in a rain forest. Over time, heavy rains have washed away much of the soil. Plant roots hold the remaining soil in place. Only the top part of the soil contains nutrients, so the roots of many rainforest trees do not grow deep into the ground. Instead, they spread outward as far as possible. Rainforest plants and animals take in and use nutrients quickly. As a result, few nutrients remain in the soil.

Rainforest animals

Like rainforest plants, rainforest animals have adapted to their habitat. In fact, most animals have bodies that are suited to living in one particular layer of the rain forest.

Nightlife

To avoid the hot temperatures in rain forests, some rainforest animals are **nocturnal**.

Nocturnal animals are active mainly at night. They spend their days resting or sleeping. They look for food at night when the weather is cool. Certain species of bats, birds, snakes, frogs, and insects are nocturnal.

This fruit bat is hanging upside down from a tree while it rests in a hot rain forest in Indonesia.

16

On the move

The Malayan tapir and the Sumatran rhinoceros are animals that live on the forest floor. Both of these animals have hard, tough hooves on their feet. The hooves help the animals walk long distances in search of food.

Canopy creatures

Orangutans and gibbons spend a lot of time in rainforest canopies. They use their long arms to swing from tree to tree looking for food. Pangolins that live in canopy trees are expert climbers. They have **prehensile** tails. Prehensile body parts are able to grasp. Pangolins use their prehensile tails to hang from trees and to balance on narrow tree branches.

The spread between a gibbon's outstretched arms may be up to seven feet (2 m) long from fingertip to fingertip.

17

Rainforest herbivores

The Sumatran rhinoceros lives only in the rain forests of Sumatra. Sumatra is an island in Indonesia.

There is plenty of food in rain forests for plant-eating animals! Different rainforest herbivores eat different foods. Some eat leaves, fruits, and flowers. Others eat branches, bark, and twigs.

Hefty herbivores

Some herbivores are small, whereas others are large. The Sumatran rhinoceros is a huge rainforest herbivore! It can weigh between 1,000 and 2,000 pounds (454-907 kg). It eats branches, twigs, bark, leaves, and fruits. An adult Sumatran rhinoceros can eat up to 110 pounds (50 kg) of food in one day!

Plant-eater pollination

Some rainforest bats, birds, and insects feed on **nectar** and **pollen**. Nectar is a sweet liquid found in flowers. Pollen is a yellow, powdery substance that plants make. Plants need pollen from other plants of the same species in order to make seeds. Bats, birds, and insects help spread pollen from plant to plant.

Moving pollen from one plant to another is called **pollination**. When animals land on flowers to drink nectar or eat pollen, some of the pollen in the flowers rubs off on their bodies. The animals carry the pollen to the next flowers on which they land, and pollination takes place. After pollination occurs, the plants make seeds, which may grow into new plants.

As this butterfly drinks nectar from a flower, pollen rubs onto its body. The butterfly carries the pollen to the next flower on which it lands.

Rainforest carnivores

Most rainforest carnivores are **predators**. Predators are animals that hunt and eat other animals. The animals that predators hunt are called **prey**.

Important predators

Predators are necessary in food chains for two reasons. First, rainforest predators help keep the **populations** of other animals from growing too large.

If too many herbivores lived in rain forests, they would eat too many plants. Predators also keep the populations of animals healthy by hunting weak, old, and sick animals. When predators remove these animals from food chains, strong and healthy animals have more food to eat.

The gavial above is a rainforest predator. It eats fish.

Second and third

A predator is a secondary consumer when it eats a herbivore. For example, a clouded leopard is a secondary consumer when it eats a deer, which is a herbivore.

When a predator hunts and eats another carnivore, the predator is a **tertiary consumer**. The word "tertiary" means "third." Tertiary consumers are the third group of animals in a food chain that must eat to get energy.

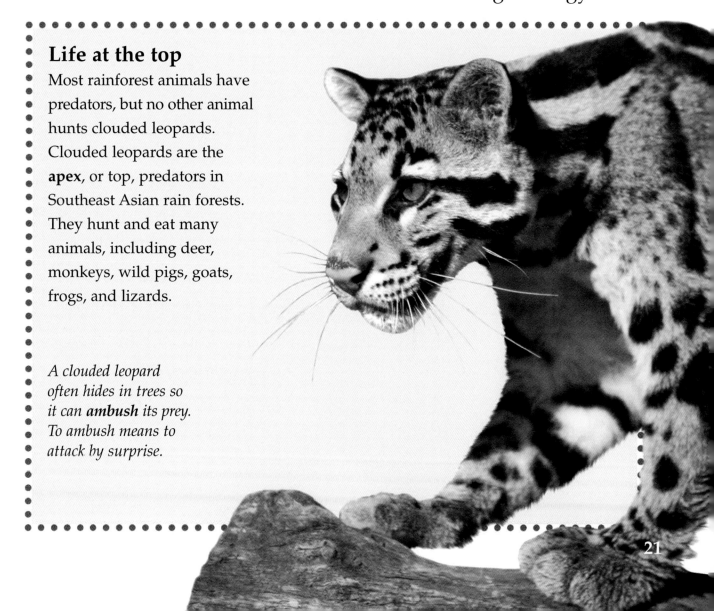

Life at the top

Most rainforest animals have predators, but no other animal hunts clouded leopards. Clouded leopards are the **apex**, or top, predators in Southeast Asian rain forests. They hunt and eat many animals, including deer, monkeys, wild pigs, goats, frogs, and lizards.

*A clouded leopard often hides in trees so it can **ambush** its prey. To ambush means to attack by surprise.*

A taste of everything!

Animals that get food energy by eating both plants and other animals are called **omnivores**. Omnivores are also known as **opportunistic feeders**. They eat any plants and animals that they can find.

Spreading seeds

Hornbills, such as the rhinoceros hornbill shown left, are omnivores. They eat fruits, insects, and snakes. Many hornbills **disperse**, or spread, seeds. They eat fruits that contain seeds. When the birds fly to new spots, they carry the seeds inside their bodies. Hornbills often drop the seeds onto the forest floor as part of their waste. Some of the seeds grow into new plants. New plants then provide more food for rainforest animals.

22

Orangutans are omnivores

Orangutans are omnivores that find food in trees. They search for food during the day. Orangutans eat figs and other fruits, as well as leaves, bark, and flowers. They sometimes eat insects and bird eggs. Orangutans walk from tree branch to tree branch or use their long arms and strong hands to swing from branches and vines. They sometimes travel long distances in search of trees that have fruit.

Eating leftovers

Some rainforest animals are **scavengers**. Scavengers are animals that eat **carrion**, or dead animals. Scavengers get energy from the nutrients in the carrion. Dead plants also contain nutrients. Over time, dead plants and animals **decompose**, or break down. Decomposing plants and animals are called **detritus**. **Decomposers** are living things that eat detritus. Decomposers take in nutrients from detritus until there are no nutrients left. In tropical rain forests, dead plants and animals decompose quickly because there are many decomposers to eat them.

*Rainforest decomposers include **bacteria**, fungi, snails, and worms, as well as termites, shown above.*

Using energy

Without decomposers, a lot of energy and nutrients in rainforest food chains would not be used. Decomposers help plants and animals at every level of a food chain by adding nutrients to soil.

Adding nutrients

Many decomposers live in soil. Their waste contains nutrients that mix with the soil. Rainforest plants need these nutrients to grow and stay healthy. When many plants grow, herbivores have plenty of food to eat. When rain forests have many healthy herbivores, rainforest carnivores have plenty of food to eat, as well.

A detritus food chain

When leaves or twigs fall to the ground, they become dead material in the soil.

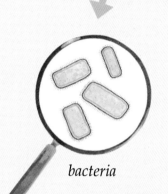

bacteria

Decomposers in the soil, such as these bacteria, eat the dead material and get some of the nutrients that it contains. They also release some of these nutrients back into the soil.

New plants use the nutrients in the soil to grow and remain healthy.

Note: The arrows in this detritus food chain are pointing to the living things that receive nutrients.

A rainforest food web

Almost all rainforest plants and animals belong to more than one food chain. Each food chain is made up of plants, one herbivore, and one carnivore. When an animal from one food chain eats a plant or an animal from another food chain, two food chains connect. When two or more food chains connect, they form a **food web**. There can be many plants and animals in a rainforest food web.

Like most rainforest insects, this green scarab beetle is part of several rainforest food chains.

A web of food

This diagram shows a rainforest food web. The arrows point toward the living things that receive food energy.

Clouded leopards eat frogs, lizards, and monkeys.

A proboscis monkey eats fruit, seeds, and leaves. It also eats insects.

Frogs and lizards eat insects.

fruit, seeds, and leaves

Rainforest insects eat plant foods such as leaves.

Rain forests in trouble

Southeast Asian rain forests—and rain forests all over the world—are in serious danger. In fact, many scientists believe that rain forests are among the most threatened areas on Earth. People pose the greatest danger to rain forests. People destroy huge areas of Southeast Asian rain forests each year. If people continue to destroy rain forests at the present rate, these forests will soon disappear from Earth forever!

Wood woes

People destroy the rain forests in Southeast Asia by **logging**. Logging is cutting down trees to sell the wood. People buy wood to make paper and to build houses, furniture, and other items. When people cut down rain forests, they kill plants and animals that cannot live anywhere else. As a result, some rainforest animals have become **endangered**. Endangered animals are at risk of dying out in the wild. If people continue to cut down Southeast Asian rain forests, many more animals will become endangered.

Clearing for crops

People **clear**, or remove plants from, huge areas of rain forests each day. Once rain forests are cleared, people plant **crops**. Crops are plants that are grown for food. Farmers keep the crops or sell them to other people.

Rainforest soil contains few nutrients, so crops grow for only a few years. When the nutrients in the soil are gone, crops can no longer grow in the soil. People must then clear more areas of rain forest in order to continue growing crops.

Harming food chains

Clearing and logging rain forests harms rain forest food chains. When plants are destroyed, herbivores have less food to eat. As a result, herbivores may not be as healthy. If there are not enough healthy herbivores, carnivores may not have enough food to eat. Some may even starve!

Some farmers destroy rain forests to plant crops of oil palm fruits, shown right. The fruits can be used to create palm oil, which many people use for cooking.

29

Protecting rain forests

This mother orangutan and her baby live in a national park in Southeast Asia. All the plants and animals that live in the national park are safe from any kind of danger.

The governments of some countries in Southeast Asia have turned certain tropical rain forests into **national parks**. National parks are areas of land and water that a government protects from harm. **Rangers** often work in national parks. Rangers are people who **patrol**, or keep watch over, the parks and make sure the plants and animals are safe.

Helping orangutans

Logging, clearing, and **forest fires** destroy the habitats of many animals, including orangutans. Some people in Southeast Asia rescue orangutans from these unsafe habitats. They bring the animals to **rehabilitation centers**. When it is safe to do so, the people release the orangutans back into their rainforest habitats.

Saving rain forests

You can help **conserve** rain forests even if you do not live near them! There are many things you, your family, and your friends can do each day to help keep rainforest plants and animals safe.

Use less

An easy way to help rain forests is to use less paper. There are many ways to use less paper. For example, write on both sides of a piece of paper instead of writing on just one side. Remember to recycle your paper. Instead of using paper napkins, use cloth napkins. Ask your parents to use cloth bags when they buy groceries. If people use less paper, logging companies will not cut down as many rainforest trees.

By using less paper, you can help protect the habitats of many rainforest animals, such as this Sumatran tiger.

Glossary

Note: Boldfaced words that are defined in the text may not appear in the glossary.

bacteria Tiny, single-celled living things that are found in soil, water, and air

conserve To protect something, such as plants or animals, from harm

energy The power that living things get from food, which helps them move, grow, and stay health

food chain A pattern of eating and being eaten

forest fire A large, uncontrolled fire that burns in a forest

habitat The natural place where a plant or an animal lives

nutrients Substances in food that help living things grow and stay healthy

population The total number of a species of plant or animal living in a certain place

rehabilitation center A safe place where animals can live if their habitats become unsafe or unhealthy

Index

animals 5, 6, 8, 9, 10, 15, 16-17, 19, 20, 21, 22, 24, 25, 26, 28, 30, 31
carnivores 10, 11, 20-21, 25, 26, 29
decomposers 24-25
energy 8, 9, 10, 11, 12, 21, 22, 24, 25, 27
food 5, 6, 8, 9, 10, 12, 16, 17, 18, 20, 22, 23, 25, 27, 29

food chains 5, 8-9, 10, 11, 20, 21, 25, 26, 29
food webs 26-27
herbivores 10, 11, 18, 20, 21, 25, 26, 29
logging 28, 29, 30, 31
nutrients 8, 9, 12, 14, 15, 24, 25, 29
omnivores 22-23
photosynthesis 12-13

plants 5, 6, 7, 8, 9, 10, 11, 12, 13, 14-15, 16, 19, 20, 22, 24, 25, 26, 27, 28, 29, 30, 31
predators 20, 21
prey 20, 21
scavengers 24
soil 7, 15, 25, 29
trees 4, 6, 7, 13, 14, 15, 16, 17, 23, 28, 31